ABOUT THIS BOOK

ABOUT WHAT HAS HAPPENED

Rights of children and young people	2
What hurts young people?	3
Why do young people get hurt?	7

ABOUT FEELINGS

Your feelings	8
Confusion	9
Fear and anxiety	10
Pain and sadness	12
Anger	14
Guilt and shame	16

ABOUT PROBLEMS

Difficulties with your family	18
Friendships and relationships	20
Difficulties with sexuality	22
Difficulties with self-esteem	24
Self-harm	25

ABOUT MAKING YOUR LIFE BETTER

Ways forward	26
Being safe	27
Taking care of yourself	30
Coping at bad times	32
Thinking and talking about your life	33
Getting support	34
Reclaiming your life	36

PLACES TO CONTACT 37

Hurting Inside

So many nights
I have stained with sadness,
staring through the dark
heard the sighing of my breath,
and I've shrunk
from another morning's stir;
for the daylight
defines my difference
and exposes me
ugly and ashamed.

Kim.

ABOUT THIS BOOK

This book is for young people who are in distress, or hurting deep inside, because of bad things that have happened to them as they have been growing up.

You might know what has caused your pain and upset. Or you may not really understand why you are in distress.

There is usually a reason why someone feels awful. It can be something that has happened recently, or even a long time ago. When we are hurt as children or young people and don't get help to deal with our pain it doesn't just go away. We keep it inside and sometimes even forget what hurt us, but the pain continues.

Sometimes the thing that causes the hurt might be physical or sexual abuse. Or it can be emotional abuse. Being neglected or deprived can leave you hurting inside, too. It can also be not having enough love and support. Love is as important as food to a child.

"I used to think I was just bad to feel the way I did. I didn't think I'd got any reason to be unhappy. My parents always bought me things I needed. But I always felt very lonely and like I didn't matter."

Whatever experiences have caused you pain in your life, the distress you feel now is real and important. This book aims to help you understand yourself and your feelings better. We hope it will also help you find ways of easing your pain, and making life better in the future.

RIGHTS OF CHILDREN AND YOUNG PEOPLE

Young people who have had a hard time don't always realise that what has happened to them is wrong and unfair. They don't know they have rights.

SOME RIGHTS CHILDREN AND YOUNG PEOPLE HAVE:

To be safe and protected from danger and harm

To be loved and cared about

To have a decent home, food, clothes and education

To have their health looked after

To be respected as a person in their own right, with their own valid feelings, thoughts and wishes

To be supported and helped to become an adult who can make their own life

---

These rights are all about making sure children have what they need to grow up safe and well. They're not about having every single thing you might want, but about things that are vital for your physical and emotional well-being.

WHAT HURTS YOUNG PEOPLE?

Children and young people should <u>NOT</u> be:
Sexually abused
Physically abused or neglected
Emotionally abused or deprived

WHAT IS SEXUAL ABUSE?

Sexual abuse is when an older or more powerful person uses a child or young person for sexual purposes. Sexual abuse can be lots of different things.

One obvious sort of sexual abuse is when an adult puts something into a child's genitals (between their legs) or bottom. (The thing could be their penis, or their fingers, an object, or their tongue.)

Stroking or touching a child or young person in sexual ways is also abuse, but it can be harder to feel sure about. Sexual touching is when the adult is touching them in order to get sexual excitement for themselves. It's not about showing affection, or comforting or looking after the child.

You might wonder how to tell whether touching is sexual abuse or not. Often the way to know this is by your feelings. If some touching **feels** wrong or uncomfortable, this is an important clue.

"I always used to give my grandad a hug and kiss when I went to visit, but I hated it when he wanted me to sit on his lap. I was too old, and he'd start 'tickling' me in embarrassing places, and breathing heavy. If I tried to get off he'd act like I'd upset him. I felt horrible, but I didn't know what to do."

You might also feel some touching is wrong if the adult seems to be trying to do it secretly, or seems excited by it. Or if you try to pull away and they keep doing it. If you aren't happy about the way someone touches you, try to tell another adult you can trust. Don't just put up with it.

Another very clear kind of abuse is when an adult persuades a child to touch the adult's penis or genitals.

Other sorts of sexual abuse might not even involve touching. For example, where an adult makes a young person watch sex, or look at 'dirty' or sexual books or films, or pose for sexual pictures. Things like making sexual comments or 'jokes' about a child's body are abusive. Talking to a child about sex to deliberately excite themselves is abuse too.

WHO ARE SEX ABUSERS?

Any adult who has any sort of sexual contact with a child or young person is abusing them. It doesn't matter who it is - someone you know or a stranger. Abusers can be parents, grandparents, teachers, youth workers, vicars, neighbours, whoever - it is still wrong. Sometimes teenagers abuse, too. This could be brothers or sisters, babysitters, cousins, or other young people. It's still abuse if the young person involved is older or more powerful.

"My brother was only a year older but he was stronger than me. My parents always took his side and I knew they wouldn't believe me if I said he was making me do sexual things with him."

We haven't been able to talk about all the possible sorts of sexual abuse here. If you have been abused in any sexual way, then this was wrong, but it wasn't your fault. If you are being abused by anyone now, you can get help to stop it.

WHAT IS PHYSICAL ABUSE OR NEGLECT?

Physical abuse means hurting a child or young person in some way. It could include hitting or punching them, kicking them, or beating them with something, or shaking, pinching, pulling their hair, burning, starving or even suffocating them.

Physical abuse is often carried out by a parent or someone who is responsible for a child. These people are allowed by law to physically punish a child 'reasonably', for example by smacking. (Some people think that even this is wrong. And being smacked a lot might upset you terribly, even though it wouldn't usually be called 'abuse'.) Teachers and other professionals who work with children are not allowed to physically punish them at all.

"No matter how I tried to be good there was always something I'd done wrong. I used to dread going home. I'd go through everything I'd done and try to think what I might get hit for."

If you have been hurt or injured by an adult (or perhaps an older brother or sister or babysitter) in any way, then you have been physically abused. Whatever 'naughty' thing you may have done, it was still wrong to hurt you.

Physical neglect can be when a child or young person is not given enough of the basic things they need, like healthy food, warmth, a decent home and clothing. Or when their health isn't looked after properly. Physical neglect could also include things like not protecting the child from dangerous things and places.

"At school I hated PE because everyone would see my old, torn underwear."

Neglect like this can have serious consequences for a young person's health and safety. It can also leave them feeling unsafe or uncared for, as if they have no value.

WHAT IS EMOTIONAL ABUSE OR NEGLECT?

Emotional abuse or neglect can be many things which cause a child or young person emotional hurt or unhappiness.

Emotional abuse or neglect includes things like:

☹ Criticising, blaming or putting a child down a lot

☹ Expecting too much of them, at school or at home

☹ Making them feel responsible for adults' problems

☹ Making them see violence, abuse or rows at home

☹ Shouting and swearing or saying horrible things to them

☹ Making them obey unrealistic or confusing rules

☹ Not showing them enough love and affection or not showing any interest in them

☹ Isolating them (hardly ever letting them be with friends or other people) or leaving them alone too much

☹ Not noticing and responding when a child is unhappy, upset, frightened or in difficulty

"My dad used to tell me that my mum was horrible and mad. Then he'd be all loving with her and saying that I was horrible and cruel to mummy. I didn't know what he meant but I felt awful."

Emotional abuse and neglect don't always get recognised as much as sexual or physical abuse. But they can be very painful and harmful to a child or young person just the same.

WHY DO YOUNG PEOPLE GET HURT?

Many young people feel guilt and shame about things that have been done to them. But adults must bear all the responsibility for how they treat children. Even if the child agrees to it, or takes money or sweets for it, the adult is still abusing them.

Young people who have been treated badly often wonder why these things have happened to them.

"I thought it must be something about me - that I was too ugly or not nice enough to love."

Sometimes parents cannot look after their children properly, even though they love them and care about them. Perhaps they are ill, or poor, or they have to work long hours, or they just can't cope. Children and young people still have the right to feel angry and let down, even if they know their parents did their best.

"I have gone over and over in my mind whether my Mum knew my Dad was abusing me. I think she probably did know some of it but she was too ill and too frightened to do anything about it."

Some young people have to bear the really painful fact that their parents (or carers) don't care enough about them to look after them properly. Some adults might be loving some of the time, but other times they stop caring how their behaviour hurts the child. Perhaps they are very angry about other things, and they take this out on a child that can't fight back.

Some people might feel good being powerful over a child. Or they decide they want their own sexual satisfaction, however wrong or harmful this is. Whatever the reason you were treated badly, it was wrong. You deserved to be loved and looked after properly.

YOUR FEELINGS

Feelings are very important. Your feelings are real and justified. Sometimes it's hard to know why you feel like you do. Feelings can seem to come out of the blue and have nothing to do with what's going on in your life right now.

What has happened to you in your life can affect what you feel both at the time and later. If people put you down a lot then you can be left feeling useless and not very confident. If people hurt you then you can feel sadness or shame or anger about it for a long time afterwards.

Sometimes you know how you are feeling. But sometimes you don't realise what's going on inside. Then your feelings can end up coming out in indirect ways. This happens a lot with feelings we try not to have.

"I know that when I keep having goes at people it usually means I'm upset underneath. But at the time I wouldn't admit it."

Some indirect ways feelings can come out include: depression, panic attacks, problems with eating, being aggressive, self-harm, getting into trouble, or taking risks.

When anything like this is happening with you it might mean you've got important feelings which need some attention.
Understanding where your feelings are coming from can help make them easier. Your feelings also need to come out in a way that you can bear, and you need to be comforted.

CONFUSION

Young people who have been treated badly often end up feeling confused. You might be confused about different things, like:

- the details of what has happened to you in your life
- what's okay and what isn't okay
- why things have happened to you
- your feelings

"I love my Dad. I feel sorry for him as well. But sometimes I hate him and want to kill him for the things he's done to me. Then I start feeling really guilty. I don't know who's bad - him or me."

It isn't surprising that young people who have had difficult experiences feel confused. Often things have happened to them which they were too young to understand at the time. Things that overwhelmed them. They might have been told confusing things. Told that something which feels wrong to them is really okay.

Try not to worry about being confused. Don't blame yourself - you have been made confused by what has happened to you. Accept that this is how it is for now. It will get better in time.

If you are mixed up about things that have happened in your life, just start with what you do know. You could write about things you remember, or make a scrap book about it. It's okay to feel lots of different things too. Just let yourself feel what you feel at different times. It might also help to talk through things that have happened to you and your feelings about them with someone.

FEAR AND ANXIETY

When you have been let down or hurt it can leave you feeling anxious or scared, even afterwards. You might have lived with a lot of fear, feeling very insecure and vulnerable or wondering when you were next going to be hurt.

It's terrifying to live in dread that someone is going to hit you, sexually abuse you, shout at you, leave you, damage or even kill you. You might also have been (or still be) scared about other things, like being worried about things happening to your brothers or sisters or your Mum, or being afraid of what would happen to you or your family if you told anyone about what was going on.

These are terrible things for anyone to be frightened about. Especially for a young person who has no-one to help them. Even if you are safe now it can be hard to shake off the anxiety you have carried for so long. It might be triggered by things that remind you of past situations where you weren't safe or secure.

Fear or anxiety shows itself in different ways. It can make you tense, jumpy or worried. Often it shows through physical symptoms, such as: shaking, breathlessness, dry mouth, heart beating fast, 'butterflies in your tummy', sickness, going to the loo a lot, aches and pains, or feeling faint.

You may not even recognise these symptoms as fear, but just think you are ill. Sometimes you can feel like you're going to die, or something terrible is going to happen. This feels awful, but nothing awful will really happen.

Fear and anxiety can also affect your eating and sleeping, or concentration. Some people have nightmares or even sometimes see or hear scary things in their mind or around them in the daytime. People sometimes develop ways of keeping their fear under control, such as continually checking things or avoiding certain places or things.

"I can't bear being in a closed room. I have to be by an open door or I start to panic. My heart races and I feel like I'm choking. I'd do anything to avoid it happening."

All this can make you think you're mad. You're not - it's a natural reaction to having had bad things happen to you. And you can get over it, in time.

WHAT TO DO ABOUT BEING FRIGHTENED OR ANXIOUS:

The first thing is to be safe. If you are in any danger in your life now, have a look at 'Being safe'. You've got the right to be safe and not live in fear any more. Even if you are not being abused now, you might still feel afraid. It can help to talk about this with someone who knows about things like abuse.

You can take control of feelings of fear or panic.

- ♥ Remind yourself there is a good reason for what is happening to you. You have got used to being frightened. Your body is reacting as if you were still in danger.
- ♥ Don't make the situation worse by panicking, feeling bad about it, or pretend it's not happening. It's okay. It will pass.
- ♥ Make sure you are not holding your breath, or breathing too fast. Try to let yourself breathe slowly and easily.
- ♥ Get comfortable and relax your body. Feel what you are touching. Feel your heartbeat. Have a look at the things around you. Listen to the sounds you can hear around you.
- ♥ Try out some things to calm and comfort yourself when you are scared. Things like putting yourself to bed or wrapped up on the sofa, listening to calming music, making a cuppa.

PAIN AND SADNESS

Young people who have been hurt or neglected have a lot to be sad about. You have been very let down. You might feel like you've never had a chance to be a child. Perhaps you have lost people you loved and needed. Or you might have always felt very alone and unloved. It is a tragedy that you have not had the love, protection and caring you need.

It can feel as if you have been injured inside, and the emotional wound has not healed up. People describe their feelings of pain in a lot of different ways, like:

hurt or sad
down, low or depressed
grieving or mourning
agony, anguish or despair
empty or abandoned
cut up or broken inside

You might be someone who often feels sad and in pain. Or you might be a person who tries to avoid feeling your hurt and sorrow, until it builds up and makes you feel really awful. How you have been treated might have left you feeling quite depressed. It isn't surprising - it's a kind of grief for all you have lost and suffered.

"Most people who know me think I'm a happy person. I always act the fool with my friends. But when I'm on my own it's like this big hole opens up and I'm so miserable."

Remember that it is natural and right to feel sorrow and pain about sad or hurtful things that have happened to you. Even if you're not quite sure why you feel in pain, there must be a good reason for it. It's not your fault if you feel awful inside. You are grieving for what has been missing or wrong in your life.

You won't keep suffering for ever. Over time the hurts inside you can heal. But it is important to give your pain the attention it deserves.

Hurt and sadness need to be taken seriously. The feelings need to be let out, a bit at a time. You might not be able to change what has happened in your life to hurt you. But letting out the anguish you feel can help ease the pain and relieve your despair.

Ways hurt and sadness can come out include:

crying

talking

playing some music that sounds like how you feel

writing (you could write a list of all the things that have hurt you and made you sad, or write a diary, or a poem)

drawing (showing what's happened to you or how your pain and sorrow feels)

It is very hard to feel sad, hurt or desperate and you might need some help with your feelings. It can seem like no-one could ever understand. But they can, and telling someone who understands about the sort of pain you are in can help you bear it and make it easier.

"Once when I was very sad I wore black clothes for the day, like I was in mourning for myself. It was really satisfying."

When you have been feeling sad and hurt it's very important to be kind to yourself and do things that feel comforting.

ANGER

It is natural to feel angry when you are treated badly, or your rights and needs are ignored. Anger is an important thing to be able to feel, because it can help you stand up for yourself.

Young people who have been neglected or abused have a lot to be angry about. Some of these things can include:

✘ *The unfairness and cruelty of how they've been treated*

✘ *The fact that no-one noticed or protected them*

✘ *Being blamed for things that weren't their fault*

✘ *Being silenced and not listened to*

✘ *Losing their family*

✘ *Feeling their life has been ruined*

Anger is not always an easy or comfortable feeling. It can be painful to be angry with people you love. Sometimes anger can feel so big that you just don't know what to do with it. Or it can just seem to well up suddenly inside, as if from nowhere.

"I seem to be wound up all the time. I end up taking it out on the wrong people and then getting into trouble."

On the other hand, some people are not able to feel angry at all, even though they have every right to be. Many people feel like it's not okay to be angry (not true!). Perhaps they have been punished, told to shut up or made to feel guilty when they are angry. They may also have been terrified by other people's anger, which came out in violent or destructive ways.

"I get angry with myself and I have to cut myself to get rid of it - all the bad feelings."

Remember that although anger can feel very powerful it is only a feeling. A feeling can't harm anyone. There's nothing wrong with anger - it's what you do with it that matters. Try some ways to let out your own angry feelings, e.g.
Going somewhere you can have a good shout

Drawing a picture of the person you are angry with, then scribbling on it, tearing it, jumping on it, spitting at it...

Writing - a few words, in thick pen - like a shout on the paper. Or write an angry letter (even if you don't send it).

Throwing things or hitting something. A dartboard is great, (you can imagine aiming darts at people you are angry with). Or you could whack the bed with a tennis racket..

Making figures out of plasticine or play-dough or clay, and then smashing them, burying them, flattening them...

Is there any safe way you could tell any of the people who have hurt you about how you feel? If not, could you talk to someone else about how unfair your life has been?

If you tend to turn things in on yourself, you could try to get some anger going on your own behalf. Ask yourself: if I let myself be angry, who would I be angry with? What particular things would I be angry about?

GUILT AND SHAME

It's sad that many young people who have been hurt or neglected end up feeling guilty and ashamed, even though they have done nothing wrong or shameful.

Guilt is when you feel like you have done something bad, as though you are to blame for something. Shame is more a way you feel about your whole self - as though you were dirty, or disgusting. Feeling like this can be agony.

Young people can feel like this because the people who have hurt them have told them that they are bad or unlovable. Or that they 'asked for it', or deserved to be punished.

Even if these things weren't actually said, being treated as if you don't matter is bound to make you feel worthless and ashamed. Also, children often blame themselves for any bad treatment they get. They assume that they must be the one in the wrong, the one who is not 'good enough' to be loved and cared for properly. The belief that things are your fault can stay with you, so that you often take on the guilt for other things, too.

"My boyfriend used to get drunk and then he would say terrible things to me and hit me. Somehow he always made me feel like I had done something to make him be like that. I'd feel so guilty and so sorry for him. It really screwed my head up, so I couldn't see what he was doing to me."

As well as feeling bad about being abused or deprived, young people may feel guilty about a whole range of other things which were not actually their fault. For example, if the abuse or neglect has come out, they might feel bad about getting someone into trouble, or upsetting their family.

If they have **not** told anyone about being treated badly, they can feel guilty about not protecting other children who might be at risk.

You can see from this how unfair it is to blame yourself - when **whatever** you do can seem wrong.

It's horrible to be weighed down with guilt or shame that you don't deserve. These awful feelings can be eased, but it might take some time. It can help to talk them through with someone who understands about abuse and neglect.

The main thing to understand is that the guilt and shame don't really belong to you. They belong to the people who have hurt you and let you down. They have shamed you and made you carry the blame. But you don't have to keep on carrying it.

Remember the list of rights we mentioned earlier. It is up to adults to make sure a child or young person receives all of this. You cannot be to blame if someone else takes away your rights. Even if you were persuaded to agree to what happened, or you were told it was your fault, you were still not to blame. Even if you took money or sweets - it still wasn't your fault!

You could try putting the guilt and shame back where it belongs - with the person who hurt you. Tell yourself it's not your guilt or shame and let yourself be angry. Have compassion for yourself and the hurt you have suffered.

"What helps me is to think to myself: What about my suffering? Haven't I suffered enough? Do I have to carry on feeling guilty forever?"

DIFFICULTIES WITH YOUR FAMILY

For many people their family is very important. Young people who have had a hard time with their family can have very strong and sometimes confused feelings about them. Their relationships with their family can be very difficult and painful.

Some difficulties with your family could include:

👎 Abuse or neglect may still be happening - see *Being safe*.

👎 Your family upset you a lot or you feel pushed out

👎 They want you to shut up and pretend nothing is wrong

👎 They blame you for things that have gone wrong in the family

👎 You and your brothers/sisters have been treated differently by your parents and turned against each other

It is important for you to find someone to talk to about how things are. There might be ways things can change. You may have a relative, a teacher or youth worker you can trust. If not, there are organisations that can help - see *Support*.

If you are old enough you might need to consider leaving home. Again, you might need help with this. Whatever else you do, you need to try and help yourself feel okay. Remember the problems in your family aren't your fault. Perhaps your parents have their own problems - you don't have to take them on.

"I tell myself I'm an okay person, whatever they think. They're the ones that are screwed up. This won't last forever. I'll be out of here one day and have my own life."

IF YOU LIVE AWAY FROM HOME

Some young people who have been ill-treated have little to do with their family once they leave home. They protect themselves by staying away from people they know will cause them pain. But it can be hard having no family.

"I sometimes get very lonely and upset, especially when I see other people with nice families and I feel like I'm different and weird. I've got my friends but I still wish I had a proper family."

Some young people want to hang on to their family, even if they still get hurt by them. Their family feels too important to lose. Often children will forgive their parents anything, because they need them so much. You can still feel this as you grow up, even if part of you hates them too.

But it can be a problem if you blind yourself to being hurt. It's important to think about your family and sort out what contact with them is right for you. You might need to think about different members of your family separately, to get clear about what you want and what is okay for you.

"My Mum couldn't hit me any more after I left home, but every time I saw her she made me feel terrible - putting down everything I was doing. So now I only see her on my terms."

Remember you don't have any obligation to anyone who hurts you or makes you feel bad. But if they are very important to you, ask yourself if it's possible for you to have any good contact with them. What would need to happen? Could you tell them how you want to be treated? Would it be better to restrict your contact to letters or phone calls, or visit with a friend? Or should you take a break from them for a while? What about brothers or sisters? Are they open to talking about how things really are and supporting you?

FRIENDSHIPS AND RELATIONSHIPS

Having good friends and relationships is important. People who you have a good time with, and who care about you. If your family aren't there for you it can feel even more important to have other people to be with.

"I hardly see any of my family. I feel my friends are my family. It's taken a while to build up, but I do feel like they are there if I need them, much more than my real family ever was."

At the same time, though, relationships and friendships can sometimes be hard for young people who have been badly treated. Things that can be hard include:

☹ *Not trusting people or letting them get close*

☹ *Trusting people too easily - even untrustworthy people*

☹ *Feeling that no-one likes you*

☹ *Being shy and finding it hard to talk to people*

☹ *Not knowing what is okay in a relationship*

☹ *Letting people treat you badly or take advantage of you*

☹ *Wanting more than people are able to give*

It's not surprising these things are difficult. Children learn about relationships from the people who look after them. If those people let you down, how can you learn properly about trusting and being close? Of course you don't want to risk being hurt any more. Or if you have been starved of the love you needed, no wonder if you end up desperate for love. That can make you want far too much too soon from relationships, or stop you realising when someone is wrong for you.

Take your time about friendships and relationships. Give yourselves a chance to get to know each other slowly. Be yourself and don't try to be what you think others want.

Don't hang around with people who make you feel bad. Trust your feelings. There are other people in the world who will respect you and be real friends to you.

You may not have much experience of knowing who to trust. Try to base your opinion of people on how they are with you and not on how you have been treated in the past.

Stand up for yourself. You have rights in relationships.

YOU HAVE THE RIGHT TO:

Be treated with respect

Set your own limits

Say what you feel and think

Say what you want and need

Decide what's important to you

Make your own choices

Not take on responsibility for other people's problems

But remember that other people have these rights too and you need to respect these.

"With my girlfriend we try to be straight about our feelings but not blame the other person for them. Sometimes it's hard but it works better being honest."

DIFFICULTIES WITH SEXUALITY

Your body is your own, precious and private to you. Your sexuality (that is, your sexual feelings and what you do with them) is your own, too. It's something to enjoy and feel good about for yourself, when and how you want to.

Sex can be a difficult subject for some young people who have been abused or badly treated. This isn't surprising, really. Sex is quite a tricky thing for most people anyway. If your body or your feelings have been hurt or intruded upon by other people, it can be more difficult for you to feel okay about yourself or other people sexually.

"I used to have sex with anyone who was interested. It didn't feel like I had any choice. It didn't even feel like it was my body."

If you have been sexually abused you might find it confusing when you are having a sexual relationship. Sex can get all mixed up with the abuse and be frightening. It can help to stop and talk about it and remind yourself of who you are with. You need your partner to be understanding and supportive.

Try to relax and take things gently around sex. There's no rush about it. Explore your own body and your sexual feelings slowly, just doing what you feel ready for at any time. Don't give yourself a hard time about sex. Remember that many people find it hard but that most problems go away on their own in time.

"I decided not to have sex with anyone for a while and just try to feel better about my body. Doing things like swimming helps."

The main thing to know about sex is that you've got rights.

SOME RIGHTS ABOUT SEX:

🖐 It's your body. You are the only person with the right to decide what you do with your own body.

🖐 It's okay to explore and touch your own body.

🖐 You have the right to choose who you have sex with and who you don't.

🖐 You have the right to explore and choose your own sexual identity - straight, gay or bi-sexual.

🖐 You have the right to say 'no' to sex or to particular sexual activities if you want to. You can also change your mind at any point about sex, and say 'that's as far as I want to go'.

🖐 It's fine to enjoy sex and not feel guilty. It's also okay not to want sex.

🖐 You have the right to protect yourself against pregnancy, HIV, etc. (e.g. using condoms, or avoiding penetration).

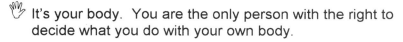

With some things it's a good idea to get some support. If you are gay or bisexual, it's good to contact other gay people (perhaps through Gay Switchboard), otherwise you can feel isolated. If sex freaks you out a lot, you could get some help to talk through the abuse or difficulties you have suffered. If you feel like doing something abusive to others, you can change this, but you do need some help. (By the way, most people who are abused do **not** go on to abuse other children themselves.)

DIFFICULTIES WITH SELF-ESTEEM

It's hard to feel good about yourself when you have been treated badly. You grow up with messages in your head about how useless, stupid, and awful you are. When things like this have been said to you, or you have been treated as if you are these things, then you begin to believe them yourself.

"I couldn't concentrate at school because of being so unhappy. I just thought I was stupid. I didn't make friends either because of not being able to take them home. I felt like I was rubbish."

Many young people end up feeling they hate themselves. They turn all their hurt and anger in on themselves. Because they haven't been loved as well as they should have been, they don't learn how to like themselves. It's very painful to feel like this.

Fortunately, it is possible to stop feeling so bad about yourself. In time, you can begin to like yourself and feel more confident.

You need some new messages to say to yourself inside. You are a worthwhile, unique person, just as good as anybody else. You are worth loving. You might not have had the chance yet to be and do everything you are capable of, but there's still time.

It's a good idea to write a list of all the good things about you. They could be things about what you are like as a person (kind, intelligent, honest, strong, funny, ...), things you are good at, or things you achieve (small things as well as big).

Taking good care of yourself also helps you feel you are worthwhile. We'll talk about this more later.

SELF-HARM

When feelings become unbearable we need to find ways of getting through. Things that take away our terrible feelings, or help us not to feel so powerless. Unfortunately, some of the things we do to cope can create other problems for us. Ways some young people cope with their feelings include:

Self-harm - cutting or hurting yourself
Alcohol - drinking too much
Drugs - using pills, street drugs or solvents
Food - starving or bingeing

When you first start to cope in any of these ways it is usually because you don't know any other way to get by. It is great that you were able to find something that worked for you. Otherwise you might not have made it at all. What you did to cope may have helped you to feel more in control. But you could start to feel like it controls you.

Young people can get a lot of criticism for things like self-harm or using drink or drugs, etc. That can make you feel worse about yourself. That's the last thing we want to do in this book. Don't give yourself a hard time for the things you have done to cope.

What we would like to do is to help you take care of yourself and give yourself more choices. Have a look at the things in the next section on *Coping at bad times* and *Taking care of yourself*. These can give you some ways to get through without harming yourself.

If you have a problem with any sort of self-harm, you could contact one of the projects listed in the back of this book. They will understand and help.

WAYS FORWARD

It can seem like life is never going to get better for you. Perhaps you are stuck in a situation where you are being badly treated. Or perhaps you are safe now but feel your life is still messed up.

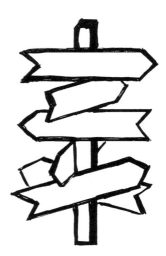

It can feel like you are never going to get over the painful feelings and problems that your life so far has caused you. Like you're going to keep hurting inside forever. A lot of people have thought this, but then found that things do gradually get better for them.

Things can be sorted out for you. You can heal up the 'wounds' inside yourself, and have a happier life. That's what the rest of this book is about - helping you to:

☺ make sure you're safe and not being treated badly

☺ take care of yourself - physically and emotionally

☺ be able to cope with your feelings

☺ think and talk about your experiences

☺ get support when you need it

☺ reclaim your life and your future for yourself

BEING SAFE

Some people reading this book may be in a situation where they are not safe. If you are being hurt (physically or mentally) or exploited in any way, that's wrong. You have the right to be safe.

You might be unsafe because of different things, like:

- You are still living with parents (or people who are supposed to take care of you) who abuse you or who deprive you of important things you need.

- You don't live with these people any more, but they still treat you abusively when you see them.

"For years after I grew up and left home my Dad still used to touch me up whenever I went to visit. I just used to pretend it wasn't happening."

- Some other adult behaves wrongly towards you, for example by making sexual advances.

- Your partner (someone you are going out or living with) is violent or is sexually or emotionally abusive to you.

- Someone is exploiting you, say by getting you to have sex with people for them to make money, or by forcing you to work unreasonably long hours.

"I was in a live-in job looking after children. They never let me out or have any time off and I was working about 18 hours a day. I hardly got any money and I didn't have anywhere else to go."

If any of these things are happening to you, or any other things which don't feel right, they can be stopped. Remember you absolutely have the right to be safe and be treated with respect and care by other people.

❦ *If you are being abused, ill-treated or exploited in some way, don't think you have to just put up with it* ❦

It can be difficult for people who have been abused to trust themselves to know when they are being badly treated later on. This is because they are still struggling to believe they have rights and that their feelings matter. And people who abuse or exploit other people can be good at persuading you that what they are doing is okay, or that it's your fault. They can seem to others like 'respectable', nice people, even though they are no such thing.

If you **feel** uncomfortable or ill-treated, then **something** is wrong. Trust your feelings. You know when you feel safe and comfortable, and when you don't. If you don't feel okay with a person or a situation, then something definitely needs to change.

"When I was about 13 I had this sports coach. He used to get me to do oral sex on him. He made me feel I was really special - I thought he loved me and would marry me. Later on I found out he did it to all the girls he trained. I felt like dirt for ages after."

If you are not sure about the rights and wrongs of a situation, you could also talk to someone else about it, to get their view.

Some situations can be changed by telling the person concerned that their behaviour isn't okay, and you're not going to accept it. You might need to say that if they carry on you'll report them, or not have anything to do with them. (Don't challenge someone if they are likely to get violent - just stay away, or get some help.)

It's easy to say "just tell them where to get off". It's a lot harder to do. Remember you have the **right** to be treated with respect. You could practise what to say first. Maybe you could have a friend with you when you have your say. Or you could write a letter, rather than say the words.

"There was this older man in the storeroom at work who used to make sexual comments every time I went down there. In the end me and my friend had a real go at him and he stopped it. He was really off with me afterwards, but I didn't care."

Sometimes it's no good telling someone not to treat you badly, because they don't take any notice. Or they might agree at the time, but later just go back to behaving in the same old way. Getting and staying away from people who treat you badly may be the only solution.

"I used to go around with this girl whose dad was really creepy. He was always looking at me and making dirty comments. I was too embarrassed to say anything. In the end I stopped going round her house any time he would be there."

It's harder to get away if the person who is hurting you is someone you love or depend on in some way. Or if getting away from them would mean losing something really important, like your job, home, school or college. Some people are afraid to get away because they have been threatened with being found and hurt if they do. In these situations you may need some help.

There are some situations which you can't sort out on your own. You need and deserve some help. There are people to talk to, and places to go if you need somewhere safe. There are organisations listed at the back of this book. Do remember, although they offer a 'confidential' service they may have to inform Social Services if they feel you or a child are at risk. You could ask about confidentiality first. Anonymous helplines could help you explore possibilities if you are worried.

TAKING CARE OF YOURSELF

Taking care of yourself means making sure you get the things you need to feel okay - both physically and emotionally. You might not have been taken care of properly by other people in your life, but you can try to take good care of yourself now.

It can be hard to feel like taking care of yourself. You might feel too angry. You might think "Why bother?" or "I don't deserve it."

You definitely do deserve taking care of. In fact, you need and deserve extra T.L.C. (Tender Loving Care), to help make up for the past. Some of this you can give yourself.

You might be angry that you haven't had the looking after you needed. You're quite justified. But don't punish and deprive yourself even more. By taking care of yourself you are saying "I'm not going to let them ruin the rest of my life!"

People who haven't had good care taken of them as children need a chance to learn to give themselves things they need and want. We're all individuals, but in general people need:

- A safe, warm, comfortable home with your own things around
- Nice food you enjoy and that keeps you healthy
- Enough rest, sleep and time to relax
- To do things with your body, like dancing, swimming, walking
- Having some fun and doing things you enjoy
- Being with people when you want, and time to yourself
- Attention to your own feelings - taking what you feel seriously, expressing your feelings, comforting yourself when you're sad

COMFORTING YOURSELF

Taking care of yourself is something to try to do all the time - part of living every day. But sometimes you need some extra looking after. When you feel sad or lonely or empty you need some comfort.

You might not have been comforted much by other people in your life. You need to find out what is comforting for you - what makes you feel warm and peaceful and cared for.

It could be things like:

Curling up in bed or on the sofa with a hot water bottle and a cup of hot chocolate

Talking kindly to yourself, like you would to a hurt child

Having a cuddle with yourself, your dog or cat, teddy or pillow

Being in the country or a park where it's peaceful and green

Having some food you love

Watching a nice video or T.V. (films for children can be really comforting); reading a good story is great too

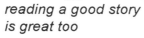

Buying yourself a little present

Playing some music that soothes and 'lifts' you

COPING AT BAD TIMES

Many young people who have been abused or deprived find they have times when they feel so awful that it's hard to cope. Sometimes your feelings can get enormous and unbearable. It's important to have some ideas for what to do when your feelings are too much for you. Here are some ideas to try:

❖ *Okay, so **don't** cope for a while. Stop trying to just carry on as though everything was alright. The world isn't going to end if you just give up and stay in bed for a while.*

❖ *Tell yourself how awful you feel. You could also write down or draw something to show what you're feeling. (Later you might want to show this to someone.)*

❖ *Don't put yourself down for what you feel. There are good reasons for it.*

❖ *Try not to panic. Terrible feelings don't last forever. They will pass if you accept them and don't fight them.*

❖ *Do something that comforts you or takes your mind somewhere less painful, e.g. listening to music, going for a walk where there's trees or water, watching TV, a warm bath ...*

❖ *It might be best to be with someone who cares about you. Maybe do something nice like going to a cafe with a friend.*

Different people find different things help them cope at bad times. When we feel really awful we can forget that we can ever feel better, or that anything can help. So it's a good idea to write a list of things which help you cope. You can look at your list when you feel rough to remind yourself. Your list could include some phone numbers of people that can help, too.

THINKING AND TALKING ABOUT YOUR LIFE

You may feel you would rather not think or talk about the things that have happened to you. It might seem like it's all too painful. Or you might feel you do want to tell someone. Most people do find that it helps them to go over what's happened to them - in their own mind and with someone else too. The important thing is to do what is right for you and at a time that is right for you.

It can be hard to talk about how you have been treated, but also a huge relief. Telling your story can be a way of saying "This is how it was and it wasn't fair and it wasn't my fault". It can ease the burden of secrecy you have been carrying and help you feel less alone. You may feel upset by telling, but it is better than having all that pain bottled up inside you. At least you can get some comfort for your pain.

Finding the words to say it can be difficult; it might be easier to write it down. You could then choose whether to show it to someone. You might have difficulties remembering everything. But that doesn't matter. It's not the details that matter but the fact that you were treated badly.

"I was afraid to tell anyone because there were huge blanks in my memory. I was afraid they would say it couldn't be true. But I told this worker how I used to feel and she was great."

If you are going to talk to someone about what has happened to you, it is important to choose the right person. It could be a friend or a relative, or you might rather talk to people who have been through similar things, or to a counsellor.

GETTING SUPPORT

Everybody needs support. Support means having people who care about you and will help you. People who take you seriously and want to know about your life and your problems.

You need different people, to give you different sorts of things. Some people can help you with practical things, like money or a home. Other people can listen to your feelings or help you with worries. Support might come from families and friends. But if you haven't got a supportive family, you've got the right to some support from people whose job it is to be there for young people.

People often feel embarrassed or ashamed about needing support. You might think you should be able to manage on your own. Or you might not want to show anyone you are vulnerable. It's understandable to feel like that if you have been let down in the past by people who should have supported you.

But it's important to reach out for support when you need it, and shows a lot of courage. It's good to take care of yourself by thinking what more support you might need.

☆ Have you got a safe, decent place to live? Do you need help with housing or other practical things, like money?

☆ Are you in danger from anyone abusing you, threatening or bullying you? Do you need help to be safe?

☆ Have you got anyone to talk to about your feelings and the things that have happened in your life?

☆ Is there someone you can contact in a crisis, if you can't cope?

☆ Have you got places to go in the day or evening and be with other people when you want to?

Do you need any support or advice about things to do with work, school, college, or your future?

 Have you got somewhere to go with worries about things like health, sex, pregnancy, alcohol, drugs or self-harm?

You might need to find out the best people to go to. In this book we can't tell you all the places to go in your own area, but we can tell you the sorts of places to look for. You should be able to find addresses and phone numbers for your area in the phone book, the local paper, or the library. Some places to try include:

Teachers, college welfare services, youth or social workers.

Young People's Advice, Information and Counselling services - these are free and there's one in most areas. Ring Youth Access (see page 37) to find out your local one.

Citizens' Advice Bureau (CAB) - can tell you about lots of things themselves, or tell you where else to go locally.

Helplines - to talk about feelings or get info. There are helplines for lots of issues: abuse, rape, domestic violence, sexuality, pregnancy, feeling suicidal, debts, drugs...

Rape and Sexual Abuse projects

GP's (family doctors) - can refer you to someone to talk to. Or you might prefer to go to a *Wellwoman Clinic, Family Planning Clinic, or Young People's Health projects*

Housing Advice Centres, Welfare Rights Advice Centres

All these places should be confidential - they won't tell anyone else your business. (unless a child or young person was being abused - they would have to report it). Ask them about confidentiality first if you want to be sure.

National Aids Helpline: 24 hours. 0800 567 123 (freephone)

National Drugs Helpline: 0800 776 600 (freephone)

National Self-harm Network: Info and campaigning for people who self-harm. PO Box 7264, Nottingham NG1 6WJ

NSPCC Child Protection Helpline: Free 24 hour helpline - counselling, info & advice for young people at risk, and those concerned about them. 0800 800 500

Refuge: Domestic violence helpline – counselling, support and help for women and children 24 hours 0870 599 5443

Samaritans: Crisis support for people in despair or suicidal 24 hours. 08457 909090.

Sexwise: Advice for young people about sex and personal relationships. 0800 282930

Survivors: For male survivors of sexual violence. PO Box 2470, London SW9 9ZP. 0207 833 3737.

Who Cares? Linkline: for young people who are or have been in Care. Freephone 0500 564 570

Youth Access: Will put you in touch with young people's support or counselling projects in your area. 0208 772 9900.